FATHI

by Nancy Farino

SAMUEL FRENCH

FOR AMATEUR PRODUCTION ENQUIRIES

UNITED KINGDOM AND WORLD
EXCLUDING NORTH AMERICA
licensing@concordtheatricals.co.uk

020-7054-7298

Each title is subject to availability from Concord Theatricals,
depending upon country of performance.

The moral right of Nancy Farino to be identified as author of this work has been asserted in accordance with Section 77 of the Copyright, Designs and Patents Act 1988.

USE OF COPYRIGHTED MUSIC

USE OF COPYRIGHTED THIRD-PARTY MATERIALS

IMPORTANT BILLING AND CREDIT REQUIREMENTS

NOTE

This edition reflects a rehearsal draft of the script and may differ from the final production.

FATHERLAND was first performed at Hampstead Theatre Downstairs, London, on 31 October 2025. The cast and creative team were as follows:

CLAIRE . . . . .Shona Babayemi
JOY . . . . Nancy Farino
WINSTON. . . . . Jason Thorpe

Writer. . . . . Nancy Farino
Director . . . . .Tessa Walker
Designer. . . . . .Debbie Duru
Lighting Designer . . . . Christopher Nairne
Sound Designer & Composer. . . . . .Khalil Madovi
Movement Director . . . . Rebecca Wield

Hampstead Theatre champions the original, presenting world-class theatre on two ever-transforming stages.

Since its earliest incarnation in a simple hut over 60 years ago, Hampstead Theatre has always attracted outstanding talent, from Harold Pinter, Mike Leigh and Tom Stoppard to Nina Raine, Roy Williams and Beth Steel – innovators and original thinkers, every one.

As one of London's leading producing theatres, Hampstead Theatre showcases the very best of what's new; taking pride in the premiere of an astonishing debut, an inventive reimagining of an existing work, or an enthralled first-time audience member. It presents plays that are ingenious, surprising and accessible.

Hampstead Theatre's state-of-the-art home is in north west London, offering West End production values – but with tickets at a fraction of the cost. Hampstead believes in thought-provoking stories that are intelligently told, leaving audiences entertained and exhilarated.

hampsteadtheatre.com

CAST & CREATIVE

SHONA BABAYEMI | Claire

Theatre work includes *BOXES* (Theatre Peckham); *Twelfth Night* (Actors From the London Stage Company, US tour); *A Midsummer Night's Dream* and *Twelfth Night* (both Shakespeare's Globe); *[BLANK]* (Donmar/Clean Break); *Rising* (Cardboard Citizens Theatre Company, UK tour); *Every Brilliant Thing* (Cockpit) and *Glint* (Theatre Royal, Stratford East).

Film work includes *Polite Society.*

NANCY FARINO | Writer/Joy

Nancy trained at the Bristol Old Vic Theatre School.

Theatre work includes *The Merchant of Venice 1936* (Trafalgar); *Twenty Something* (Old Red Lion, Edinburgh Fringe); *Homegrown* (National Youth Theatre); *Richard II* (The Willow Globe, Powys, Wales); *Blessings* (Camden People's Theatre) and *Dare You Say Please* (King's Head).

Short film work includes *Should I Fall Behind* and *Midnight Ride.*

Television work includes *Amadeus*; *Masters of the Air*; *Anatomy of a Scandal* and *Silent Witness.*

JASON THORPE | Winston

Theatre work includes *The Merry Wives of Windsor* and *School for Scandal* (both RSC); *Nation, Morning to Midnight, The Hour We Knew Nothing Of Each Other, His Dark Materials* and *Peter Pan* (all National Theatre); *Where There's a Will* (ETT); *Under Glass* and *Greed* (both The Clod Ensemble); *Beasts and Beauties* (Hampstead Theatre); *Absurd Person Singular* (Leicester Curve); *The Hound of the Baskervilles* (Peepolykus/Duchess); *What the Butler Saw* (Vaudeville) and *Perfect Nonsense* (UK tour).

Film work includes *The Banishing, Holmes and Watson, Fast and Furious 6, The Nine Lives of Thomas Katz* and *Jack and the Beanstalk: The Real Story.*

Television work includes *The Inheritance, The Famous Five, Sister Boniface Mysteries, The Girl, Miss Scarlett and The Duke, Flack, The Witcher, Curfew, Sense8, Call the Midwife, Agatha Raisin, Poldark, The Delivery Man, Holy Flying Circus, Little Dorrit, Coming of Age, Primevil, Trial and Retribution, The Queens Sister, Wire in the Blood, Sir Gadabout* and *Goodbye Mr Steadman.*

TESSA WALKER | Director

Recent work includes *Mrs Bibi* by Waleed Akhtar (Audible); *Run, Rebel* by Manjeet Mann (Pilot Theatre Company, UK tour; *Bright Places* by Rae Mainwaring (Birmingham Rep/UK tour); *Northanger Abbey* adapted by Zoe Cooper (Orange Tree/UK tour) and *Biscuits for Breakfast* by Gareth Farr (Hampstead Downstairs).

She was Associate Director at Hampstead Theatre from 2021 to 2023 where she directed *Ravenscourt* by Georgina Burns and *Big, Big, Sky* by Tom Wells.

Other productions include *Symphony of Us* by Paul O'Donnell (Coventry Cathedral, Coventry City of Culture) and *The Glad Game* by Phoebe Frances Brown (Nottingham Playhouse/UK tour/film).

As Associate Director at Birmingham Repertory Theatre productions included *Circles* by Rachel De-Lahay, *Back Down* by Steven Camden, *The Whip Hand* by Douglas Maxwell, *Looking for John* by Tony Timberlake, *Folk* by Tom Wells and *The Quiet House* by Gareth Farr.

DEBBIE DURU | Designer

Recent theatre work as a designer includes *woman.life.song* (Birmingham Opera Company); *A Christmas Carol* (Northern Stage); *Bright Places* (Birmingham Rep); *How I learned to Swim* (Roundabout/Brixton House); *Re:Discover* Festival (Streetwise Opera); *Beneatha's Place* (Young Vic); *Run, Rebel* (Pilot/Mercury); *Ravenscourt* (Hampstead Downstairs); *The White Card* (Northern Stage); *Two Billion Beats* (Orange Tree); *A Song Project* (Royal Court); *Cake* (Theatre Peckham) and Josephine (Theatre Royal, Bath).

Work as Costume Designer includes Now I See (Theatre Royal, Stratford East); Twice Born (Scottish Ballet); Romeo & Juliet (Almeida) and Alice in Wonderland (Brixton House).

Work as Associate Set Designer includes Get Up! Stand Up! The Bob Marley musical (Lyric); Dick Whittington (National theatre) and Mandela (Young Vic).

Debbie was the winner of the Black British Theatre awards for Theatre Design 2023.

CHRISTOPHER NAIRNE | Lighting Designer

Previous work for Hampstead Theatre includes *Blackout Songs* (shortlisted for both the 2023 Offies and the 2024 Profile Awards). Christopher was also an Offies finalist in 2020 for *Preludes* and won the award in 2016 for *Teddy* (both Southwark Playhouse).

Other theatre work includes *Groan Ups* (Mischief Theatre, Vaudeville/UK tour); *Hold On to Your Butt*s, *Jeeves & Wooster in Perfect Nonsense* and *The Last Temptation of Boris Johnson* (all UK tours); *Boy Parts* (Soho); *The Real Ones* (Bush); *Farewell Mister Haffmann* (Park); *Samuel Takes a Break...* and *This Beautiful Future* (Yard); *Tom Fool* and *Mayfly* (Orange Tree); *The Legend of Sleepy Hollow*; *The Beautiful Game* and *A Little Princess* (all The Other Palace); *Jerusalem* (Watermill, Newbury) and *Lionboy* (Complicite, world tour).

Opera work includes *L'Agrippina* (Barber Opera); *Madame Butterfly*, *Jephtha* and *Macbeth* (all Iford Arts); *Belshazzar* (Trinity Laban Conservatoire); *Vivienne* (Linbury Studio, ROH); and *La Bohème* (OperaUpClose – 2011 Olivier Award Winner).

KHALIL MADOVI | Sound Designer & Composer

Khalil is an award-nominated music artist, composer, writer, actor and filmmaker. In 2024 Khalil was nominated for a Black British Theatre Award for his sound design work.

Theatre work as a sound designer includes *Two Gentlemen of Verona* (RSC); *Why a Black Woman Will Never Be Prime Minister* (Camden Peoples Theatre); *G* (Royal Court); *Red Pitch* (Bush/Soho Place – Offie Nomination for Best Sound Design); *No More Mr. Nice Guy* (Broadway Theatre, Catford/UK tour); *Brenda's Got a Baby* and *Metamorphoses* (both New Diorama); *Divine* (Arts Ed); *This is What the Journey Does* (Old Vic, as part of One Voice: HOME series) and *The Poison Belt* (Jermyn Street).

Work as a composer and sound designer includes *Animal Farm* (Theatre Royal, Stratford East/Leeds Playhouse/Nottingham Playhouse); *Revealed* (Belgrade Theatre, Coventry and Tobacco Factory, Bristol); *Gone Too Far!* (Theatre Royal, Stratford East); *Sound Clash: Death in the Arena* (Pleasance One, Edinburgh Fringe) and *Can I Live?* (Barbican).

REBECCA WIELD | Movement Director

Rebecca is a London based movement director and artist. She trained at The Royal Ballet School and danced with English National Ballet, before training as an actor in 2015. Rebecca has an MA in Movement Directing and Teaching from the Royal Central School of Speech and Drama in 2023.

Work as Movement Director includes *Guys and Dolls* and *Duet for One* (Frinton Summer Season); *Musik* (Wilton Music Hall); *Persona* (Saatchi Gallery – Lumen prize nominated 2024); *Biscuits for Breakfast* and *Ravenscourt* (both Hampstead Downstairs); *Roberto Zucco*, 2nd year BA Actors, (Fourth Monkey); *Hamlet*, BA (Hons) CDT 2nd year Bridge Project, (Royal Central School of Speech and Drama) and *Painting* (The White Bear).

Work as Choreographer includes *Pickled* (National Film & Television School); *I'm King*, Drag Performance (RVT, Ivan - If - A – Boy); Assistant Choreographer, *Addams Family*, 2nd year BA Musical Theatre (London College of Music).

Choreographer, director, writer, performer – Lockdown Palladium, live-streamed.

Work as Intimacy Coordinator includes *Me to You* (National Film & Television School).

CHARACTERS

WINSTON – 50s

JOY – late 20s

CLAIRE – 30s

MATTHEW – recording only

WOMAN'S VOICE – recording only

VOICEMAIL – recording only

ACKNOWLEDGEMENTS

As I write this, I'm filled with the dreadful anxiety of knowing I have most likely forgotten to thank someone. In all honesty, I owe far too many people far too much thanks for making this possible. The following is an attempt at a (non exhaustive) list of people I am truly very grateful for...

This play is the product of years of R&Ds, collaboration and having to explain to my family what R&Ds are. Ben Jacob Smith – thank you for being the play's champion from day one and for your fervent belief in me and it. This wouldn't be possible without you – endless Guinness on me. The main R&D for *Fatherland* was made possible by RAW Inventive whom I am very grateful to, alongside Jules Head, Daisy Edgar Jones, Yohanna Ephrem, Leon Finnan and NT Studios. Thank you to Alfie Jones and Lynton Appleton for their work on the project in its first days, and to anyone I blackmailed into doing Zoom readings.

Huge thank yous to Jen Davis, Rhianna Biggs, Alice Hamilton, Roy Williams and Greg Rippley Duggan and the entire team at Hampstead Theatre for supporting my writing and making this the perfect home for *Fatherland*.

Thank you to my agent Jessi Stewart for all your patience, support – mainly emotional – and hard work throughout.

Thank you to the team at Concord for publishing the play. My first published play! I can't believe how many times it contains the word 'poo'.

Thank you to Jason Thorpe for taking a chance on a slapdash R&D and playing Winston perfectly since. I will continue to write problematic men for you as long as you'll fancy playing them.

Thank you to Shona Babayemi for your strong, beautiful Claire.

Thank you to Tessa Walker for simply being the best director and most lovely person to work with. I couldn't be more grateful for the insight, hard work and humour you've brought to this whole process. Thank you for bringing it all to life so brilliantly.

Lastly, I want to thank my partner, my friends and my family for their unwavering support throughout the truly misguided career choice of being an actor-writer. I'm so lucky to have such wonderful people to invite along to my plays and ask them to laugh loudly. Thank you.

For my Dad. You are one of a kind.

1.

(**JOY**'s breathing. The ins and outs of troubled sleep. Birds flock in swirling formation, leaving for warmth. Deep breaths become shallow.)

(**WINSTON**, alone, in the front seat. He drums on the steering wheel impatiently.)

WINSTON. My name is Winston Smith and only good things happen to me. My name is Winston Smith and only good things happen to me. My name is Winston Smith and only good things happen to me.

(Headlights. Ahead, in the distance, he sees a small frame in a cloud of smoke, perched on the pavement. He strains over the wheel to see.)

(It's **JOY**.)

(Underslept. Overtired. And very fucking cold.)

(A determined white light in the distance heading towards her. She blinks hard. The light grows stronger and cuts through the grey. Dazzling, almost.)

Joy?

Joy!

(She rubs her eyes 'til she sees stars. The grunt of an engine.)

WINSTON. Joy – move out the way!

> *(The light has a loud voice. One she knows.)*

Joy for fuck's sake!

JOY. Dad?

WINSTON. I want to park there! Can you hear me?

> *(She nods.)*

There! I want! To park! There!

> *(She moves; he parks. A flurry of neck craning, swearing and rolling up windows before he gets out. **JOY** dashes the joint on the floor.)*

JOY. Dad. You're here.

WINSTON. Hello pidge. Did I hit anything?

> *(He gets out. Or tries to. Beat.)*

JOY. What are you doing here?

> *(Beat.)*

WINSTON. Stinks of Indian Hemp around here.

Oh god. What's that – have you been on the Indian Hemp again?

JOY. Don't call it that.

WINSTON. Nasty stuff that. Indian – sorry. Dope. Nasty stuff that dope.

Is that a latte?

JOY. No. Dad –

WINSTON. Looking at it, I think I did actually scuff that bonnet.

(Beat.)

JOY. Dad. You're here.

WINSTON. Hello sweetheart. You look. Rustic.

JOY. Did I know you were coming?

WINSTON. I text.

JOY. Oh

(Beat.)

WINSTON. Let's go inside.

(Beat.)

JOY. My flatmate. They're on a Zoom.

WINSTON. On a what?

*(Like a camera coming into focus, **JOY** takes in what **WINSTON** arrived in.)*

JOY. Is this yours?

WINSTON. Did I not tell you? I bought a bus.

JOY. …

WINSTON. I bought a big old fuckin' bus.

JOY. You bought this?

WINSTON. You didn't tell me you had a flatmate.

JOY. You didn't tell me you had a bus!

WINSTON. Used to be a school bus. I renovated it. She's been my project for quite some time now. Started in Covid, forgot about her for a bit and then finally finished her off. Yep. Tore out the seats. Put in new ones. Installed a poo pipe. Which is for.

JOY. Got it.

WINSTON. There's a bed in the back. And portable chargers and lights you can turn red. In fact. I turned them red and now I can't get them off of red. So there are red lights. Like some kind of sex bus.

JOY. Dad.

WINSTON. I'm not allowed to say sex bus anymore?

Not that I'll be having any s-e-x on the old sex bus. Nicole hates it. Bloody popemobile.

(*Beat.*)

JOY. Sorry. When did you text?

WINSTON. I need a latte.

JOY. Dad.

2.

(A cheap little office somewhere on the outskirts of Bristol.)

CLAIRE. Winston?

WINSTON. Yes. Hi.

CLAIRE. Good afternoon. Well evening.

WINSTON. Ha. Yes. I suppose. Good evening.

CLAIRE. Hi.

WINSTON. Hello.

CLAIRE. You alright?

WINSTON. Yes. All good.

And you?

CLAIRE. Fine thank you. Shall we?

WINSTON. I'm just waiting here for a Mr – Sarfati.

CLAIRE. Pleasure.

WINSTON. Oh. You. You're. Hello!

CLAIRE. Do you want to take a seat?

WINSTON. I'm sorry.

CLAIRE. That's okay.

WINSTON. Don't have my glasses on.

CLAIRE. There's fine. To sit.

WINSTON. Was thinking about getting laser. Lasic.

CLAIRE. Do you want to tell me a bit more about why you're here?

WINSTON. Where they put the lasers in your eye. But it doesn't stop colour blindness – fix it, I mean – because that's a neurological problem. In your brain. Brain damage. Which I have.

CLAIRE. You're here because you have brain damage?

WINSTON. No. I can't tell the difference between red and green because I have brain damage – colourblind – damage.

CLAIRE. Right.

WINSTON. Makes apples very confusing.

CLAIRE. Sure.

So I have a bit of information from the online form but I'm going to need you to expand on a few things to better my understanding/

WINSTON. Are you new?

CLAIRE. Why do you ask?

WINSTON. Well, you're young. Younger. Younger than other people – people who are older than you – if I'm correct in assuming –

CLAIRE. You are correct. I am, in fact, younger than people who are older than me. Insightful as that may be, I'm guessing the question you'd actually be asking is whether I'm as qualified as anyone else to see you through your current situation. / Well, that's why I want to ask you a few questions now.

WINSTON. I never said you weren't. And it's not because you're a woman.

CLAIRE. Right.

WINSTON. I love women.

CLAIRE. Fantastic.

WINSTON. Didn't see you on the website. That's all. Then again. Glasses.

CLAIRE. Well, that answers my first question. You found us through our website? Okay. And is there any particular reason you chose us?

WINSTON. Because of the lovely decor.

CLAIRE. Can you tell me more about your case?

3.

(Tiny overpriced coffees in hand. **JOY** *and* **WINSTON** *face the bus.)*

JOY. Two sisters and two brothers. So four?

WINSTON. Four. Well, half.

JOY. God. What are they like?

WINSTON. The woman who messaged me – the sister – the half – she's an idiot. Her whole page is full of Gary Barlow and awful artwork her kids have done – seriously they must be cognitively challenged –

JOY. Dad.

WINSTON. – and – this huge message – that she sent to me. Wait. First message she sent was telling me she thinks we might be – you know – and then I reply – da da da – and the next day I get a message from her saying "send this to twelve people or else Facebook will steal your data".

JOY. Oh god.

WINSTON. Very dim. She's youngest. Thirty odd. Works at a leisure centre. In Swansea. Then there's Anthony, David and Lorraine.

JOY. Our Lorraine?

WINSTON. No. Another one. Probably made it easier for him.

JOY. Jesus.

WINSTON. She contacted me a couple of months ago, saying she's done all this family tree malarky online.

JOY. Do you think Nanny knew?

WINSTON. No. I don't know. I mean she never said anything. This woman seems to know tons about my father. And our whole lineage. And it's nothing like I thought.

JOY. Is it legit?

WINSTON. Looks like it. She said she paid a company to do it. All looks verified and – turns out – there's a long line of us – going back for years and years – in County Mayo.

JOY. Where's that?

WINSTON. God. Joy. Come on. This is where we're from!

JOY. I'm sorry. I didn't know I was from there 'til about / two seconds ago.

WINSTON. It's in Ireland.

JOY. No. I know it's in Ireland. But where?

WINSTON. The. The. West.

JOY. Are you sure?

WINSTON. For years all I had to go back on was my mum's side. And I knew nothing about where my father came from or his father or his father's father. I felt like I had to be this – this – this patriarch for the whole family. I always wondered about the men that came before me. A whole side of me – of us really – that I didn't know.

(**WINSTON** *paces circles.* **JOY** *vapes.*)

JOY. That coffee is really working.

WINSTON. And now we know.

JOY. And now we know.

WINSTON. I've always felt a bit Irish.

JOY. Have you? How?

WINSTON. So cynical, Joy.

JOY. I'm just. Digesting. Yes. It's great. And very cool. Do we have any family there still?

WINSTON. That's what I want to find out.

JOY. Well. Yeah. It's cool. We should go one day.

WINSTON. We are.

JOY. That's the spirit.

WINSTON. Today.

JOY. Hm?

WINSTON. Mum said you'd been all mizzy.

JOY. You spoke to Mum?

WINSTON. She said you've been all mizzo.

JOY. Can we just say miserable?

WINSTON. So we're going today.

JOY. We. We?

WINSTON. You've been all miserable, Joy. Which actually is very ironic. Because.

JOY. Yes.

WINSTON. So I thought let me come and take my baby on the trip of a lifetime.

JOY. I mean. That's so. Let me check my –

WINSTON. It's the holidays. No kids to teach.

JOY. Yes. Yes. It is.

WINSTON. What else have you got planned?

JOY. Now there must be something.

WINSTON. Well. Cancel it! We're going to Mayo. We're going to Mayo. We're going to Mayo.

JOY. Okay. Okay. Okay. Well. Let's just. Did you book flights or.

WINSTON. There's the thing.

JOY. Oh no.

WINSTON. What?

JOY. I don't like when you have things. Historically, whenever you have a thing it's a whole. Thing.

And I think I know what this thing is and I'm not sure I like it.

WINSTON. Come on, Joy.

JOY. Don't you need a special licence to drive this?

WINSTON. Yes m'aam. All done.

(She approaches the bus with caution.)

JOY. Jesus.

WINSTON. I'm thinking I'll rent it out after our trip. Consider this a test run. It's like a traveling Airbnb. You know, if someone wanted a holiday in Dorset – I'd drive Buster to Dorset and then –

JOY. Buster?

WINSTON. The bus.

JOY. Of course.

Is it. Are they. Safe?

WINSTON. Joy.

JOY. It's incredibly impressive, what you've done. All of this. It really is. But I'm sorry – you're not a / professional –

4.

CLAIRE. Professional life coach?

WINSTON. Yes. I offer life coaching services. Have done for years and inevitably, that attracts some types. You know. Well. People who might've been knocked off course. You know.

People who are in need of tools that can help them get back to themselves. Or a better version of. And most of the time that delivers incredibly fulfilling life-changing results.

CLAIRE. Could you say more about that? Examples, perhaps?

WINSTON. Examples. I'd have to consult my records.

CLAIRE. Okay.

WINSTON. I mean. Well. Briefly. One of my clients was going through a divorce, very messy, and now, well, he lives in Alicante now. So that speaks for itself really.

CLAIRE. Mm. Any more?

WINSTON. I'm very selective with my clients. But I can check.

CLAIRE. I see. Okay. We can circle back to that. I think it would be the most helpful to use this time to discuss your services with this particular client. Starting from November of last year?

WINSTON. Yes, so started in November. And that went up until. April. Of this year.

CLAIRE. Any supporting material or notes that you might have would be really useful.

(*He holds up a notebook.*)

Have you been asked to provide copies of this to anyone?

WINSTON. I scanned something across to someone, yes.

CLAIRE. Great. I know it might be difficult to remember in full but as much detail as you can please.

5.

JOY. Please can you get someone to check? Like an expert or –

WINSTON. I took it to a garage and they said it looked perfect. More than perfect.

Think of the history of this thing – all the happy little children it carried to and from school. They didn't worry about it being 'safe' they just hopped on with their jolly little lunches, ready for adventure and learning and let themselves enjoy the ride/

JOY. Well. I'm not an Enid Blyton character. And I don't know how up for it – ready for this, I am –

WINSTON. Joy. It's safe. I'm your dad and I wouldn't let you on it if it wasn't safe.

I've planned it all. Its perfectly easy. Bus, ferry, bus.

JOY. Fucking hell.

WINSTON. You could sound more enthused.

JOY. There's just a lot happening at once.

WINSTON. Ah sure, that's how life works. Nothing happens for ages and then lots of things happen at once. Fucking annoying, really. But you have to ride the wave – catch the bus – literally – join the conga line whilst the things are happening!

JOY. Well. I don't know. I've been. Can you not go with Nicole?

WINSTON. She's no sense of adventure. She's so Ovaltine sometimes, honestly. And I want to go with you. My Joy.

JOY. I can't.

WINSTON. Why not?

JOY. You have to arrange these things in advance.

WINSTON. What a boring way to live life.

JOY. I'm fine with being boring.

WINSTON. I'm not!

JOY. Now isn't a great time.

WINSTON. I've come all this way!

JOY. Well, I'm sorry?

WINSTON. Don't be sorry, be spontaneous! Come on. I want you to come. You have to come. Please. Just get on and have a look!

> *(The door swings open with a wheeze and* **JOY** *steps on.)*

Oop – ignore that. Going to sand that down. Careful there. Recognise that? I had that in my old flat. That too – that bit of art – tat – art. In fact, most of my stuff is in here – Nicole doesn't like my 'bachelor pad' items in the house. And the lights. Have you seen the lights?

JOY. The lights are nice.

WINSTON. Told you it was nice.

So. Come on. What do you think?

JOY. How long would it take? Dad?

6.

CLAIRE. Winston, please.

    (A beat.)

WINSTON.   I didn't anticipate you being quite so. Thorough. You don't mind, do you? Well.

    (**WINSTON** *kicks off his shoes.)*

You don't mind, do you?

CLAIRE. Well.

WINSTON. Good to let your feet breathe.

7.

*(**JOY** and **WINSTON** drive out of London on the bus – **JOY** wincing at every sharp corner or tight squeeze.)*

JOY. Can you keep your eyes on the road please!

WINSTON. Calm down. So dramatic. How are the kids?

JOY. Little shits.

WINSTON. Ha. What kind of stuff do you do with them?

JOY. Oh. Games. Lots of games.

WINSTON. Go on then.

JOY. Hm?

WINSTON. Show us a game.

JOY. No thank you.

WINSTON. Come on.

JOY. They involve standing up. And moving.

WINSTON. You've not got any sit down games?

JOY. You only sit down when you're dead. Well. Not dead. There's a game called 'splat' that involves you shooting each other and if you get shot you sit down but one of the parents said it promotes gun violence. So we don't play that anymore. Well, we did a version that involved magic fingers and then falling into a deep sleep. Which in turn you could say promotes groping and Rohypnol.

WINSTON. Brilliant. I mean I bet you're brilliant at it. And they're paying you well?

JOY. Yeah.

They've all got stupid names. Not stupid but. Mist. Quincy. Wolf.

WINSTON. Wolf?

JOY. Wolf.

WINSTON. Child cruelty that.

> (*Beat.*)

Hannah's just had her baby.

JOY. Oh. Yeah. Think I saw on Instagram. Is it a boy or a girl?

WINSTON. She's a little girl. Called Amelia.

JOY. That's a nice name.

WINSTON. Ugly thing, truth be told.

JOY. Dad.

WINSTON. I'm joking! Anyway, all babies are ugly. You – god. You were like some medieval gargoyle –

JOY. Gargoyle.

WINSTON. I'm serious. I was scared for you to start speaking – thought you were going to only talk in riddles or something.

Anyway, Amelia is lovely. Well. She will be. She'll grow into her face a bit more. You'll see her soon anyway – Auntie Joy – Half Auntie Joy – well sort of step –

JOY. Yeah. Definitely.

> (**JOY** *fiddles with the radio to no avail. The dial limply hangs off its base.*)

> (**WINSTON** *taps the side compartment revealing a collection of CDs. She rifles through the stack.*)

WINSTON. How's your mum?

JOY. Good. Yeah. She's doing well.

WINSTON. That's great. Really really great.

JOY. She's got surgery in a month or so.

WINSTON. Fantastic. Good to get it. Booked in. Is she able to keep her – keep them both – as a pair – as in is it a single mas-mas-mas or a double – or will they –

JOY. Single.

WINSTON. That's good. Less. Uh. Invasive. Shame to split the gang up but. Hey. She'll be absolutely fine.

JOY. I know.

WINSTON. So will she get a new one moulded on/ or rock the asymmetric –

JOY. Can you not connect your phone?

WINSTON. On the bluetooth? No.

JOY. God. These are.

WINSTON. All Nicole's. Only woman alive to not have an iPod.

JOY. No one has an iPod.

WINSTON. You know what I mean.

> *(He drains the last of his coffee from the cup and in doing so spills the remainder on his beige trousers.)*

Oh fucking hell!

JOY. Oh the lid –

WINSTON. Yes the lid! That's the last fucking time I try and save the environment – I mean it – tell that little German to get the fuck back in school because the big corps are still pissing oil in the seas and I'm being forced to drink out of a coffee cup made of fucking leaves –

JOY. Think she's Swedish.

WINSTON. Fucking bollocks.

JOY. Pull over and change?

WINSTON. I think I have some spares – somewhere in my bag I don't know –

JOY. I'll do it! Don't you – you (look away)

WINSTON. Anything?

JOY. No. Why did you not bring spare trousers/?

WINSTON. I wasn't planning on shitting myself, Joy. Okay?

JOY. Do you want to go back and change?

WINSTON. No.

JOY. Do you not have any pyjama bottoms?

WINSTON. No. I'm free when I sleep.

JOY. Lovely.

WINSTON. It'll dry soon, I suppose.

(*More silence.*)

And how's your sister?

JOY. She's good too.

(*A pause.*)

WINSTON. She still seeing Terrin?

JOY. Taheen.

WINSTON. Oh yes. Course. Of course, they could've come to Mayo, too.

JOY. I think this would be her worst nightmare.

WINSTON. I think so too.

Well, that's all the housekeeping done. Now we can really talk. Our time. On the road.

Together.

> (**JOY** *puts in the CD. Shania Twain plays. Silence.**)

Joy. I have to say. I always thought he was a bit of an asshole.

JOY. Taheen?

WINSTON. No. Lovely chap. Your one.

> (*Beat.*)

JOY. You said you liked him.

WINSTON. Did I? Well, I had a gut feeling.

JOY. Right.

> (**JOY** *turns the music up.*)

WINSTON. Life's all about picking apart the losers from the winners. Takes a while to fine tune that sense.

> (*She turns the music up.*)

And we learn from every interaction – every relationship –

> (*She turns the music up.*)

Being vulnerable is key. Despite the knock backs.

> (*She turns the music up.*)

Joy.

JOY. Shania.

---

* A licence to produce *Fatherland* does not include a performance licence for any third-party or copyrighted recordings. Licensees should create their own.

8.

CLAIRE. Matthew. Tell me about him.

(**WINSTON** *reads from his notebook.*)

WINSTON.   Matthew. Aged twenty-eight. Lives with parents. His job – works in sales. Had done since graduating from – can't read that – it wasn't one of the good ones. Average university with a 2:1 in Geography. Hence working in sales. Struggling with motivation. Recently single. Hence living with parents. Feels passionate about – at first, "dunno", when pushed, "football I suppose". No prior experience of life coaching.

CLAIRE. Anything more?

WINSTON. He's got a dog called Miffy.

Happy?

CLAIRE. May I see? This is everything from the first session?

WINSTON. My firsts tend to be pretty brief.

CLAIRE. Did you get any insight in to how he was feeling at this time?

WINSTON. Unmovitated.

CLAIRE. Is there anything else you can tell me about this session?

WINSTON. I was just collecting the facts. I have to work with the facts of his circumstance.

CLAIRE. So, no?

WINSTON. Not really.

CLAIRE. Nothing at all?

WINSTON. Miffy dies. Spoiler.

CLAIRE. Your second session was?

WINSTON. Two weeks later.

CLAIRE. Any contact in between?

WINSTON. No.

CLAIRE. Okay. So November 22nd.

WINSTON. We spoke about second hand smoke theory.

(*A beat.*)

It's a study which I've turned into a method of upgrading your own life.

Based on the idea – 'you are the sum of who you surround yourself with.' Surrounding yourself with good, successful people begets a good, successful life. So the study – won't go into who did it and where and when – but essentially; if a close friend of yours smokes, you are sixty-one percent more likely to be a smoker. Make that a friend of a friend and you're twenty-nine percent more likely to smoke. And if a friend of a friend of a friend smokes, the likelihood is seventeen percent. Sorry. That says eleven. Eleven percent.

Obviously, I'm not talking about smoking here. It's more about how easily influenced are you to pick up on someone else's bad habits? Comprimising who you are, da da da and so forth, on a larger scale. Say if your partner is a vegetarian saxophonist you'll most likely end up listening to jazz and eating falafels. Pretty harmless in the grand scheme – I find falafels particularly dry but that's beside the point – but do you compromise your own ambitions? If your partner is someone who is afraid of risk-taking and adventure – your own dreams will be compromised by that persons fear. Etc. Etc. If you spend enough time with 'smokers', you can become a 'smoker'.

That's just a summary. I invited him to consider if he was surrounded by any smokers.

CLAIRE. And was he?

WINSTON. We didn't get round to that in this session. I can skip ahead –

CLAIRE. No, no. That's alright.

WINSTON. Apologies if you smoke. It's just an analogy.

CLAIRE. All good.

WINSTON. But you don't smoke. I can tell. You don't look like you smoke. You've got good teeth and nails.

CLAIRE. Whitening strips and manicures.

WINSTON. Really? Wow. How long did you smoke for?

CLAIRE. Too long.

  (Beat.)

9.

(A lone snowflake zigzags from the sky onto the windshield.)

JOY. It starts with hands – I see hands – my hands – white cold gripping the handles of a pram – handles? The part you push.

at first I don't know it's a pram but

then i hear crying

there's a baby inside a really tiny tiny baby and i think its mine

i wasn't sure

all i kept thinking is i have to keep this baby warm

its little baby lips are going to go blue

so i wrap it up super warm and i'm looking for somewhere to take it inside

and then – then – i look up and everyone around me – they all have their own babies too and they all seem to know me – nods and waves and smiles

"Hi, Gilda!"

And I'm saying hi back?

it's all very quaint

i follow them

to a coffee shop

and outside this coffee shop there are rows and rows of prams like a sea of prams

theres like thousands of babies outside on the street

they're not all my babies god

they all look the same – Kinder wrapper blonde babies – this is the point I realise I'm probably blonde too –

all the other mothers start to go inside – to get a coffee and a a a fuckin' – strudel – yeah, strudel

just leaving the babies!

I don't want to leave the baby

but they're all doing it

apparently, we do that here

so I kiss the baby, leave the pram, and head inside.

And i just i just have this feeling there's something I need to do

that time is running out

and I must remember what I've forgotten

people were getting logs too i don't know where the fucking logs were coming from but i

was tryna get them too

i didn't even get to eat my strudel

i feel as if i need to be somewhere really badly

remember remember remember

oh fuck!

And just when it's about to hit me –

This old lady passes me – almost into me – big red cheeks like something from a children's book – she stops me and says

Det finns inget daligt vader, bara daliga klader!

and somehow I understand her

There is no bad weather only bad clothes.

i wake up and google the phrase

in english

i only dream bilingual

and it does exist

prams are left outside – good for the immune system
and respiratory stuff and ultimately makes for a much
nicer coffee shop experience

a whole creed of people from birth prepped primed
and *ready* for winter

And I'm – I'm –

10.

JOY. Can we stop? Can we stop?

WINSTON. I've not scheduled in a stop.

JOY. I didn't schedule in this. Whole thing.

WINSTON. Spontaneity, Joy.

JOY. Okay. Then I spontaneously need a wee.

WINSTON. There's a toilet on board. With a fully functioning poo pipe.

JOY. I know about the pipe.

WINSTON. I'm going to take every opportunity I can to say the words 'poo pipe'. Why wouldn't I?

JOY. You've got me there.

>   (**JOY** *fiddles with her vape.*)

WINSTON. Your thing. It's flashing.

JOY. It's run out.

WINSTON. Gosh you're very OCD about that thing.

JOY. You can't say that because I don't actually have OCD and it's offensive to people who actually do –

WINSTON. Fine. You're very anal about that thing. Now you just made me say the word 'anal' for no reason. If I see services we'll stop. If it's not too out the way.

JOY. Thank you.

>   (**WINSTON**'s *phone rings. 'Claire Office'*
>   *announces the phone.*)

WINSTON. Not now.

JOY. You can take it, I don't mind.

WINSTON. No, no, no. Later. But thank you, gracious master.

> *(The sat nav lady soothingly instructs a turn.)*

Oh god, everything at once. Shut her up, will you?

JOY. You sure?

WINSTON. Yeah, I know it from here. Just needed to get out of Central. You know, Nicole calls her my other woman.

JOY. The sat nav or 'Claire Office'?

WINSTON. Good one.

> (**JOY** *turns off the map lady, her vape flashing at her in vain.*)

Seriously. Those things.

JOY. I know. Bad for you.

WINSTON. No. They make you look like a twat.

If you're going to do it. Do it properly. I'd rather kill myself with some big old Cuban than a pathetic stick of watermelon.

JOY. Well if they sell cigars at the services I'll make the switch.

WINSTON. Atta girl. I used to smoke a pipe. Just a regular pipe. Not a...

JOY. Go for it.

WINSTON. Poo pipe.

> *(A beat.)*

So. Are you doing any hard drugs?

JOY. Dad.

WINSTON. You can tell me.

JOY. What would you call hard drugs?

WINSTON. God. I don't know. Heroin?

JOY. No. I'm not doing heroin.

WINSTON. I was just asking – you know – because.

JOY. Ah, yes. Vapes being the notorious gateway into heroin that they are.

WINSTON. Low people – miserable, as you prefer – they often find themselves doing drugs. That's all I'm saying.

JOY. I'm not doing miserable people drugs. If anything the times in my life where I've been the happiest, I've done the most drugs. And even then, I didn't dabble in heroin.

WINSTON. Okay! That's great! I'm just glad I'm not one of those parents that you have to hide things from. You can tell me anything. We can talk about drugs. Or sex /

JOY. I would genuinely rather kill myself/

WINSTON. Or heartbreak.

I remember my first heartbreak. I looked her up on Facebook the other day actually.

Thankfully, her life looks terrible. But I remember that pain. God. The pain. I've had my fair share.

(Silence.)

You ever see the musician?

JOY. He moved to Cornwall.

WINSTON. And the alcoholic?

JOY. Dunno.

WINSTON. And then. Well, he's moved out. What happened there then?

JOY. How about. I just talk to you about it when I'm ready?

WINSTON. Okay.

JOY. Okay.

(**JOY** *exhales. A pause.*)

WINSTON. But will you ever really be 'ready'?

JOY. For fucks sake.

WINSTON. 'Ready.'

(**JOY** *doesn't respond.*)

This young guy I was life coaching –

JOY. I'd really prefer/ not –

WINSTON. This young guy, Matthew – he's really been through some shit –

JOY. I don't think you're meant to say his name –

WINSTON. Okay. Then. Fine. Mr Hudson. He's –

JOY. So what you've done there is essentially give me his full name –

WINSTON. Well I could be lying! Can you just let me –

JOY. Right.

WINSTON. It was a break up that really sent him to a dark place. Amongst other things.

11.

WINSTON. I encouraged him to talk to people. When you're getting a coffee, talk to the people making it, people in the queue, talk to all of them. Find out new things.

Don't worry about interrupting anything – just go for it.

What's that say? Piercings. Yes. Whenever I see someone with a piercing, as a rule of thumb, I will always ask them if it hurt.

CLAIRE. If it what, sorry?

WINSTON. If it hurt. Or when they got it. Or why they'd want a slab of metal halfway through their nose. I'm never without conversation when I see someone with a piercing. Um. Yep. Homeless people. Talk to homeless people too. They're fabulous – got fabulous stories I mean. Often sad. Very sad. But stories you could make a very sad fabulous film about. I know all the homeless people in my area. The idea of integrating these smaller conversations into your life and how they will only enhance the more meaningful, important conversations you have.

CLAIRE. And how did he respond to that?

WINSTON. Very well.

CLAIRE. Did you get the impression he was lonely?

WINSTON. Do you reckon they picked crucifixion because it's the most aesthetically pleasing symbol?

CLAIRE. Pardon?

(He gestures at her necklace.)

WINSTON. I just imagine, you know, what if they had hung him? Would you have a noose around your neck – figuratively – or, you know, a bludgeon or a sword on a chain – if they had. Done that. To him.

CLAIRE. Oh. Him as in Jesus?

WINSTON. The mind boggles as to what symbolism they'd have chosen if the chair had been around back then. Everyone would have to pray in front of a giant plug socket or what if he had a nut allergy and thats how they did him in – would we all gather around some sort of macabre cashew statue and wear macadamias round our necks –

CLAIRE. Winston.

WINSTON. Just a thought.

CLAIRE. It's not a cross – a crucifix.

WINSTON. What is it then?

CLAIRE. It's a T.

WINSTON. T for?

CLAIRE. For my father.

WINSTON. ...Terry?

CLAIRE. No.

WINSTON. Do people often confuse it for a cross –

CLAIRE. No. Do you need a break?

WINSTON. No, I'm alright.

CLAIRE. I'm having a coffee.

WINSTON. Bit late.

CLAIRE. Would you like one?

WINSTON. No, be up all night. You don't like the questions, do you?

CLAIRE. No more than you like mine.

    (A beat.)

WINSTON. I'll swap you.

CLAIRE. You do realise I'm trying to help you? You're paying me to help you?

WINSTON. I don't need help, surely you can concede this is all somewhat. Over the top.

CLAIRE. They're trying to –

WINSTON. Hang on. Was that one of your questions?

CLAIRE. No. That wasn't a proper question.

WINSTON. Sounded like one. My turn.

CLAIRE. I'm not partaking.

WINSTON. Who's that in your screensaver?

(*A pause.*)

CLAIRE. Colin Firth. You acknowledged the claim back in July and you've not spoken to anyone since then about representing you?

WINSTON. Not really. The guy who did my divorce referred someone but he was useless and charged me royally for a six-minute phone consultation. He also had a lisp. Couldn't stand him.

CLAIRE. Okay.

WINSTON. They've got branded pens and cucumber water in the waiting room. Divorce felt like a bloody spa retreat.

CLAIRE. Did you tell him anything about the allegation?

WINSTON. Hardly. Allegation sounds very serious.

CLAIRE. Did they read the claim? Did you share any materials with them?

WINSTON. Now you've had two. Why did you start smoking?

CLAIRE. My parent's were big smokers. Ashtray in the bathroom.

WINSTON. Handy.

CLAIRE. Materials?

WINSTON. No.

CLAIRE. Running between different firms can make you look desperate and panicked –

WINSTON. Hardly running –

CLAIRE. I suppose you need shoes on to run.

WINSTON. I knew you minded.

CLAIRE. And the claimant's team? F&A? Have you had any further contact with them?

WINSTON. No.

CLAIRE. They're good. I used to work with a few of them.

WINSTON. What happened there?

CLAIRE. Nothing. I was an associate there and now I'm not.

WINSTON. Why?

CLAIRE. Just life. Your letter of acknowledgment of the claim. Did you do that independently?

WINSTON. Yes. I still have a question.

Can you tell me something about him.

(He gestures at the T necklace.)

(A beat.)

CLAIRE. He had this beard.

This big beard.

This big beard that just seemed to grow overnight, not to stubble – to full bush in honestly a number of hours. He didn't like himself with all the hair so he'd shave and I remember he'd always have a cigarette halfway through shaving. He'd look like one of those cabaret acts – with the half-man half-lady – with a cigarette hanging out his mouth. That's funny. I've not thought about that in ages.

WINSTON. That's a nice way to be remembered.

CLAIRE. Yeah.

12.

JOY. I'm not really sure you should be telling me any of this.

WINSTON. Who are you going to tell?

JOY. No one. But it's client – confidentiality. / I wouldn't want my therapist talking about me.

WINSTON. Well, he's no longer my client. / You have a therapist?

JOY.	WINSTON.
You fixed him?	You're seeing a therapist?

JOY. Yeah.

WINSTON. That's good. Hey. That's cool.

> *(A beat.)*

And how is that?

JOY. Oh sure it's like the Graham Norton show. Very charming and anecdotal. We just laugh and laugh and laugh.

WINSTON. What kind of things do you talk about?

JOY. Nothing. Honestly.

> *(Beat.)*

I've not been sleeping well.

WINSTON. Need to see a chemist for that. What else?

JOY. I don't know. Things have just been tricky.

WINSTON. Tricky how?

JOY. Just a lot at once. It's fine. It's mainly the sleep.

WINSTON. Insomnia?

JOY. A bit. Sleep paralysis.

WINSTON. Are we not all somewhat paralysed when we sleep?

JOY. Seeing things. Almost a bit like a nightmare but not being able to move or speak or do anything.

WINSTON. Fuck the chemist, let's get you an exorcist. What things do you see?

JOY. Weird shit. Dunno.

WINSTON. Oh darling. What do you think that's about?

(*Silence.*)

Sleeping alone? Do you miss him?

JOY. No.

WINSTON. Perhaps subconsciously. Dreams can really tell us things.

JOY. You think?

WINSTON. I get these awful dreams I'm bathing a baby, supporting the neck, keeping their head above the water and suddenly the phone rings – it's one of those telephones with the cords – you're too young – and for some reason, against all better judgement, I get up and answer the phone. And I can't hear whoever's on the other line so I hang up and sprint back and save the baby but then the phone rings again. Back and forth until I wake up. I'm sorry, I was trying to make you feel better but I think I could've chosen a better dream.

JOY. What does that dream tell you?

WINSTON. Fuck knows.

(*A pause.*)

JOY. I was really really really stupid.

WINSTON. No, Joy. You're actually very bright.

JOY. No, I was. He was a bad bad person. And I think it was very clear and I was very stupid. Sometimes I see him when I'm asleep and it's like I watch myself in slow motion about to make all those stupid decisions again and again and –

(Call from 'Claire Office' blares on the handsfree.)

WINSTON. Bollocks – sorry! Sorry. Stupid thing. Go on.

JOY. I don't want to talk about it anymore please.

WINSTON. I'm sorry. Come on. I'm listening. Tell me more.

(She gives nothing.)

13.

*(A light sheet of settled snow on the car
bonnet.)*

JOY. I have one where I'm Persephone. The Greek lady.
Girl. I don't eat the pomegrantes.

One where I'm Morana and I don't find out about
my lover lying to me. I don't poison him. I don't get
banished.

One where I'm Skadi and I hunt for fun not for revenge.

I'm Persephone's mother, Demeter, and I try gentle
parenting instead of starving the land. I'm Frau Perchta
and I replace my knife with needles and knit myself
back to warmth.

I am the brother from that film and I don't go through
the wardrobe and I'm allergic to turkish delight.

I don't shoot arrows at the sun or poison or kill.

I read the small print.

I am good and happy and barefoot and oblivious and...

14.

*(**JOY** fills the car with watermelon smoke. A '90's girly pop anthem plays.*)*

WINSTON. Warmer. You're getting warmer. Not hot.

JOY. I give up.

WINSTON. Don't want to hear any of that. Come on.

(A beat. Reluctantly –)

JOY. I'm a White British male actor, over forty but under sixty.

WINSTON. That's right.

JOY. And I'm not Jude Law or David Tennant or Daniel Craig.

WINSTON. Yes. I mean, no. You're not. Stop guessing and ask more questions.

JOY. I tried! Okay. Have I. Have I ever won an Oscar?

WINSTON. Hm Maybe. Don't think so.

JOY. This is what I mean. The game doesn't work if you don't know/ about the person you've picked –

WINSTON. Fine! No! You haven't won an Oscar!

JOY. Thank you. Have I ever been in a Christmas film?

WINSTON. Oh god. Well. I think you might have been. Sure. Why not. Yes.

JOY. Am I brunette?

WINSTON. Yes.

---

* A licence to produce *Fatherland* does not include a performance licence for any third-party or copyrighted recordings. Licensees should create their own.

JOY. Am I Hugh Grant?

WINSTON. No. You're very hot with that one though! Boiling hot.

JOY. I give up.

WINSTON. Stop giving up after four questions! I got Barack Obama and I didn't give up even after –

JOY. Thirty seven questions.

WINSTON. Exactly!

JOY. Oh shit.

WINSTON. What?

JOY. Ferry is going from Holyhead, right?

WINSTON. That's the one.

JOY. I think they're postponing it –

WINSTON. What do you mean postponing – they're not postponing anything –

JOY. Weather warnings.

WINSTON. Very funny.

Let me see. Oh for god's sake. Zoom in. Zoom! Fucker. What the –

JOY. They all just say delayed. Did you not check the website before?

WINSTON. Yes, I checked it!

JOY. Well. It'll be fine. Let me see if they've got anything later.

WINSTON. Fuck.

(**JOY** *laughs sharply.*)

What?

JOY. Nothing. It's just. This is just/

WINSTON. Can you keep looking?

JOY. Do you remember when we saw *Happy Feet* together?

WINSTON. What's that?

JOY. It's a film. About penguins.

WINSTON. I don't know. Clearly, I don't know anything.

JOY. We went for my ninth birthday. You were going to take me and Molly Aldersley. But we got to the cinema and there was some kind of mix up, you – we hadn't booked it and you asked if we could sit in the aisles and they said no because of health and safety –

WINSTON. Bullshit rules.

JOY. So we had to see something else. You said it was a better film anyway. So we got loads of pick 'n' mix and got like completely sugar high. Like hyped the fuck up.

And went to see the only other film showing that day which was... *The Pursuit of Happyness*.

The one about Will Smith and his son becoming homeless and sleeping in public toilets and his wife leaving him.

WINSTON. Great film. /God. No memory of seeing it then.

JOY. I mean, yeah. But I was nine so I probably didn't appreciate it all that much. On my ninth birthday we watched *The Pursuit of Happyness* and Molly Aldersley fell asleep.

WINSTON. Great message in that film. Never give up. No matter what. Arguably a great lesson to learn on your birthday.

JOY. Mm.

Mum was pissed.

WINSTON. No, she wasn't.

JOY. Yeah. She was.

> *(The CD reaches the last track and they sit in*
> *silence for a second before it loops back.)*

There's one tomorrow morning. Or we can head back and reschedule.

WINSTON. We're not rescheduling. We'll just grab some food and sleep here.

JOY.   It might be nicer. I don't know. Later. We can properly plan it then. Maybe a day trip another time –

WINSTON. Joy. I didn't give myself splinters fitting a pull out bed for nothing.

JOY. What did you do it for then?

WINSTON. What?

JOY. Nothing.

> *(**JOY** googles hotels nearby.)*

WINSTON. You were very hot just before. Do you want to keep guessing?

15.

CLAIRE. No. So you definitely don't have anything for the sixth?

WINSTON. Nope.

CLAIRE. So that week of the sixth?

(**WINSTON** *shrugs.*)

Do you remember the reason?

WINSTON. He went skiing.

CLAIRE. Right.

WINSTON. Or had the flu.

CLAIRE. Do you remember which of the two?

WINSTON. I'll have it somewhere.

CLAIRE. Did you talk out of session time often?

WINSTON. Only to arrange.

CLAIRE. So he told you in advance?

WINSTON. He emailed.

CLAIRE. Winston.

WINSTON. Or text.

CLAIRE. Winston, you're making this really hard.

WINSTON. You're asking me to remember the minutia of a conversation from months ago/

CLAIRE. Yes. That's exactly what someone in my position would need you to do in order to help you here.

WINSTON. In case you haven't noticed, I'm not as 'younger than other people' as you are. Can barely remember what I had for breakfast.

CLAIRE. Your breakfast isn't suing you.

WINSTON. Best sentence you've said all day.

CLAIRE. Can you please stop?

I have been trying to help you. However there are multiple inconsistencies in your timeline. I'm hearing a lot about your various methods and approaches – which yes, I do need to know – but nothing about Matthew. His progress, what he said and how he felt, how he responded to your service. I'm not sure whether you have this information and you're choosing not to disclose it or whether you really do have no idea about a client you were speaking to for six months.

Either way, it doesn't bode well for your business or your case or you as a self proclaimed empath. From your many remarks and musings and and and bartering – just general time wasting, I'll assume you're aware that this firm is in fact only really equipped to deal with minor driving offenses and definitely not something of this scale. Paired with the complete lack of information, it's not something I feel we, I, can take on. Sorry.

WINSTON. This scale?

CLAIRE. They're not going to settle, Winston.

WINSTON. What do you mean they're not going to settle?

CLAIRE. They're not going to.

WINSTON. Have they said that?

CLAIRE. No, but they will. Their team are good – expensive – and good, and I don't believe they'd hire someone of that calibre to settle like this, so soon. The family are wealthy – far too wealthy for any sense of financial loss to impact their claim. Their claim for compensation being something that they firmly believe will help to to to justify or lessen the anguish and pain and loss that they feel you have caused them/

WINSTON. I've not –

CLAIRE. I'm not expressly saying that you have. But they think you have. And they have money and a great team and realistically – if this – this, excuse me – this clusterfuck of information is all you have to fall back on, without any liability insurance, then I'd say they have a fair fucking chance. Sorry for my language.

WINSTON. I was told it would settle outside of court.

CLAIRE. By who? Winston, they're suing you for negligence and currently you're not providing anywhere near enough reason for me to dispute that claim. It would be a waste of time for me to apply for settlement.

WINSTON. So. So. So if it doesn't settle. What happens?

CLAIRE. Look, I don't know what to tell you here. It could. But, giving my professional opinion, I'd find someone at a bigger firm. I don't see this being the easy way out you thought it would be. Try the other place again. Put the lisp to one side because, well frankly, you need to. I'm sorry I can't help more. If you don't mind. They'll be wanting to lock up soon/.

WINSTON. I can't go there. Or Osborne James. Or Insight...

CLAIRE. Sorry?

WINSTON. I can't go to F&A. Or Osborne James. Or Insight. Or any of the ones that appear on the first two pages of a Google search.

I've not picked here – here – I mean, seriously, if Ryanair did legal – or you, despite you being surprisingly far more competent than the font on the website would indicate anyone here is, out of choice.

CLAIRE. You could look into a 'no win, no fee' arrangement –

WINSTON. I think you just gave the eulogy for any chance of me finding that.

CLAIRE. Then I'd suggest you weren't in any position to have been wasting my time like this. I'm sorry.

(Beat.)

WINSTON. No, I am. Really. I mean it – you are competent. I can see your little degree poking out of that box there. You should really hang that up. You're probably very wasted here. I didn't mean to waste your time.

CLAIRE. I'm not sure if any of that was a compliment, but thank you.

WINSTON. It was. I am. Well. I'm sorry. I'm sorry, aren't I? Oh god. Here we go. What can I do for you to help me? Is there anything that I can do?

CLAIRE. I'm not looking to be bribed.

WINSTON. I didn't mean a bribe. I mean. I don't know. What if. What if I did have more?

CLAIRE. More money?

WINSTON. More information.

CLAIRE. What?

WINSTON. What if I did. Have more.

CLAIRE. More evidence?

WINSTON. Evidence sounds so serious. No. Just more – materials – that might show that I was helping him.

CLAIRE. What do you mean? Winston, if you've failed to disclose – knowingly failed to disclose any more material/ then that in itself is –

WINSTON. I've not failed to disclose anything. They don't have a right to police everything I do and say and think – every utterance noted down and torn apart and inspected./ It's Orwellian! It's just come to me that I may have more –

CLAIRE. It is a contempt of court to alter or conceal information with the intention/ of preventing full disclosure of said information –

WINSTON. Oh come on. It's my information! It's personal. /No one has a right to anything!

CLAIRE. It's not personal. It's business. He hired you for a service./ And legally, they do.

WINSTON. Do you know what else is mine? My underwear. It's like someone coming in to my underwear drawer and parading my my my unmentionables all over the place. Do they have a legal right to that?

CLAIRE. Oh my god.

WINSTON. It's no different to someone rifling through your personal phone – seeing your personal messages and just broadcasting them about –

CLAIRE. You may want to sit down for this/ –

WINSTON. I'm not talking about China stealing your data or whatever the –

CLAIRE. Getting a little conspiratorial here –

WINSTON. What? I'm not allowed to say China? China China China China China!

>   (*Beat.*)

I'm disclosing it now. To you.

CLAIRE. I'm not the – disclosing what?

>   (*Beat.*)

WINSTON. Recordings. The last three sessions.

CLAIRE. You have recordings of the sessions?

WINSTON. Only the last three.

CLAIRE. Oh my – First of all – did you have consent? To record?

WINSTON. Well.

CLAIRE. You'd have needed proper consent.

WINSTON. I wasn't planning on sharing them.

CLAIRE. Clearly not – these should have been shared weeks ago –

WINSTON. Aha! He didn't give me consent to share. I mean I didn't have any consent. So. Surely, surely, there's a loophole somewhere in there?

CLAIRE. No. There's surely not. Why on earth did you making recordings?

WINSTON. I thought we were making good progress! We had been through the basics – all of my usuals and in the last leg I really thought we were stumbling across a new territory – I was coaching from here – from the heart! I really was invested in helping him and I thought that these recordings would come in useful.

CLAIRE. For what?

WINSTON. I was going to write a book.

(*This sits flimsily in the air.*)

CLAIRE. I don't know whether to pretend I didn't hear any of that. For your sake.

WINSTON. You said I needed more information!

CLAIRE. Not like this.

WINSTON. Please.

CLAIRE. Winston. I don't even know where to begin.

WINSTON. Begin with helping me.

CLAIRE. No. I've said no. Please just go.

(*Beat.*)

WINSTON. Sorry. Enjoy your parking fines.

(**WINSTON**, *like an injured animal, puts on his shoes. It takes a while.* **CLAIRE** *fiddles with her not-crucifix.*)

CLAIRE. Do you have them with you?

16.

(In the queue for the tollbooth, M6.)

WINSTON. Somewhere in the glove thingy – box –

JOY. Nothing.

WINSTON. You're looking with one hand!

JOY. There's nothing there.

WINSTON. Sure I had some change somewhere.

JOY. You can pay by card.

WINSTON. You sure?

JOY. Mm.

WINSTON. Who are you texting?

JOY. I'm not. I'm playing a game.

WINSTON. What game?

JOY. Rollercoast Tycoon.

WINSTON. What's that?

JOY. It's where you have a rollercoaster park – you design it and build it yourself and then you have to manage it.

WINSTON. That doesn't sound fun.

What's that there?

JOY. What? Oh. That's sick. If you get really big rollercoasters, people spend more money to go on them, which is good, but you also get a lot more thrower-uppers, so you have to hire more cleaners.

WINSTON. The game is cleaning up sick?

JOY. Only part of it.

WINSTON. When I was your age, we used to work all day and then play games that were fun. But you lot you have fun all day and simulate actually working. Your games are fake labour –

JOY. Pick up sticks. You taught me to play pick up sticks. That's fake labour.

WINSTON. Did I?

JOY. Yes.

WINSTON. But there's skill involved there. You have to pick up the sticks with a certain /*je ne sais quoi* –

JOY. – you know it is actually more complex –

WINSTON. not just sloshing sick around –

JOY. Okay, games over.

WINSTON. Love a good game of pick up sticks.

(*A beat.*)

You know. You're the only one who really calls me.

JOY. Not true. Claire Office calls you.

WINSTON. Joy.

JOY. Yes?

WINSTON. Do you know what the word facetious means?

JOY. She called you a bunch of times.

WINSTON. I mean your sister doesn't call me. Well, she does, but she always has to get on the tube about five minutes in.

JOY. She's very busy.

WINSTON. Very. Seems to spend half her life on the underground. Little mole woman.

JOY. She does the tube thing to me too.

WINSTON. Really?

> (*A beat. They roll up to a toll booth.*)

Seventeen quid?! Seventeen fucking quid!

JOY. I can pay?

WINSTON. It's fine.

"Toll fees go towards road maintenance" – fucking sure they do. It's like driving on a fucking flapjack.

Go on, take my money then. Greedy bastard. Go on take it!

> (*He inserts his credit card – rather, he jams it in. The machine splutters and hisses at it.* **WINSTON** *stabs at buttons. The machine dies.*)

What the fuck?

JOY. What's happened?

WINSTON. Fucker has eaten my card!

JOY. Oh shit.

WINSTON. Bastard!

JOY. Press the seek assistance button.

WINSTON. I can't – whole things gone to sleep ! Wake up! Wake the fuck up!

JOY. Why would it do that?

WINSTON. I don't know! Divine fucking intervention?

> (*A car beeps behind them.*)

It's broken! Go round!

JOY. Sorry. Do you have money? Other money on you?

WINSTON. Yes. I've got another card. But I want this one back!

JOY. You can order another one online.

WINSTON. And how long will that take?

JOY. I can do it for you now. I think we should let other people through –

WINSTON. Google if this has ever happened to anyone else ever or if I'm just the protagonist of a fucking parable.

JOY. Okay. Okay. Just keep driving.

WINSTON. Surely someone must work here! I'm getting out.

JOY. No – there's people –

> (**WINSTON** *exits and marches through lines of cars.*)

WINSTON. Excuse me! Excuse me! I need some help here!

> (**JOY** *watches him through the windscreen. Crawls into the backseat. Waits.*)

17.

(Once transient and fleeting, snow begins to settle, pitching camp around her.)

JOY. *Help me! Help me!*

There's a woman in the distance – on her knees and crying – reaching out her hand for me to help her

she's not properly dressed for this weather

i called out to her but she didn't see me, i got closer and closer and – she's beautiful with this long black hair – i thought perhaps she was hurt – so i step nearer and reach out to her and just as its too late i notice the veins in her hand

And we touch

i can't remember getting home but i am

i'm so cold

i run a bath

in the bath, under a candle's light, I noticed my skin turning blue – I was raised on stories about them –

the Yuki Onna – snow women, hunters

i bundle myself up in every cloth – sheet – cover in the house

i Amazon prime an electric blanket and hot water bottles and ear muffs and fleeces

i take the kettle straight off the fire and pour the boiling water all over myself

Nothing is warming me

i use every bit of furniture in the house for firewood

Mother will be angry

the nineteenth-century Amazon Prime delivery driver arrives by horse and cart

still cold

my skin translucent, hair black, lips blue

he forgot to ask me to sign

stood in front of me, he looks so warm

it's pulling me in

so so so warm

so i grab the back of his neck and take it – all of his warmth – i inhale it – drain him like a Capri-Sun - fucking devour it and for a moment i feel warm again

he crumples in front of me

fuck

No no no

what have I done?

there's nothing but this empty skin bag at my feet now

and I am cold again

No no no

what's happening to me?

i need to leave, to be alone

what if I get them? Mother and father and grandmother – what if I –

i'm so cold –

they can't see me like this, i'm a – a – a

18.

(**JOY** *asleep in the backseat,* **WINSTON** *drives up front. Eyes dart between his phone and the road.*)

(*They wind through a village somewhere outside Holyhead. The sound of wind. A crackle of static. The sky rumbles knowingly, angry.* **JOY** *blinks awake.*)

JOY. Fuck was that?

WINSTON. Nothing. Come and chat.

JOY. I'm tired.

WINSTON. You were dribbling for a moment there. And then – like a a a one of those – Dysons! Like a Dyson you hoofed it back up with a snore.

JOY. Stop watching me sleep.

WINSTON. You want to play a game?

JOY. No.

WINSTON. Joy, come on. No more naps.

(*She rolls back over to try and sleep again. Silence. Too much silence.* **WINSTON** *punches on the CD.*)

19.

(The click of a tape starting. **CLAIRE** *and* **WINSTON** *in transfixed listening mode. Halfway through the second recording.)*

WINSTON. *(Recording.)* My name is Winston Smith and only good things happen to me. My name is Winston Smith and only good things happen to me. I say that or think that every day, multiple times a day. It's my mantra. I want it to be your mantra. I mean. Say your own name. Don't say my name. Because that's my name.

> *(***MATTHEW*** laughs lightly. As he listens, we can hear him alive and breathing down the other line. Horribly intimate.)*

(Recording.) I speak this out loud and it works like magic. The word mantra actually comes from a sanskrit word meaning charm or spell. It's always good to know where words come from. This is besides the point, but, write that down – etymology –

> *(We hear the scratch of pen on paper.)*

MATTHEW. *(Recording.)* E-t-

WINSTON. *(Recording.)* E-t-y-m-ology. Knowing where words come from – makes you a much more interesting, well-rounded individual. Even just saying the word etymology has made me feel better about myself.

> *(***MATTHEW*** laughs.)*

(Recording.) But it is. Like magic. So wake up and speak it. Tell the world how your day is going to go. Because. Let me tell you. We attract what we put out. I'll say that again. We attract what we put out. And this

doesn't mean you know the whole lighting incense and having a crystal up your arse –

>   (**MATTHEW** *laughs again.* **WINSTON** *laughs too.*)

(Recording.) No but seriously, it's about intent. Intention.

MATTHEW. *(Recording.)* Intention.

WINSTON. *(Recording.)* Yes. That's right. That's why and how it can feel like everything is fucking up at once – one thing after the other. Like an avalanche of fuckery. And that's not surprising. If you're feeling shit you'll likely attract more shit. And so it goes on and on. And you don't have to be feeling actively shit, Matthew, it can just be that you're not actively feeling good. Try to feel good. If you're not trying then you might as well just give up. It's also why I try not to be too much of an empath. I won't sit and suffer with you – or anyone – I'm going to help you take positive action and feel good. I won't watch *Children in Need* but I will donate. Well. I'll think about donating. You know?

MATTHEW. *(Recording.)* Mhm.

WINSTON. *(Recording.)* What intention can you set for the next week? Well, two weeks until we speak next?

MATTHEW. *(Recording.)* Um. I want to keep up going to the gym?

WINSTON. *(Recording.)* Great. Yes. I make the intention to look after my wonderful body and prioritise my health.

>   (**MATTHEW** *echoes the affirmation.*)

MATTHEW. *(Recording.)* Look after my wonderful body and prioritise my health.

WINSTON. *(Recording.)* Lovely. Anything else?

>   (*He thinks. We hear him breathing.*)

MATTHEW. *(Recording.)* Maybe to like. Maybe to tell some people that I love them? Just. You know. Yeah. Appreciate people a bit more.

WINSTON. *(Recording.)* To show gratitude to the many special people in my life. Hmm. Let those intentions sit with you.

Well. Lovely stuff, Matt. I'll speak to you in a couple of weeks. You're doing great.

MATTHEW. *(Recording.)* I am?

WINSTON. *(Recording.)* Yes. Keep up the good work. Speak to you soon.

MATTHEW. *(Recording.)* Thank you. Goodbye. Bye.

> *(The recording beeps. We hear* **WINSTON** *pacing.)*

WINSTON. *(Recording.)* April 2025. This recording will feature on themes of community and collective –

> *(The sound of a woman's voice shouting about shoes on the stairs.)*

(Recording.) Nicole – Nicole – I'm about to have a session – can you – thank you.

> *(He sits back down again. The tones of an outgoing call. Which beeps through to a generic* **VOICEMAIL**.*)*

VOICEMAIL. *(Recording.)* You've reached the O2 voicemail. The person you're calling is unavailable. Please leave a message after the tone.

WINSTON. *(Recording.)* Hi, Matthew. It's Winston. I've got eleven in the diary for us. Calling you at eleven o six. Ring me back. New statistic. You could be laughing sixty-five percent more of the time. Call me.

Nicole – I can still hear that!

(We hear him pacing.)

(The tones of an outgoing call. Which beeps through to a generic **VOICEMAIL.***)*

VOICEMAIL. *(Recording.)* You've reached the 02 voicemail. The person you're calling is unavailable. Please leave a message after the tone.

WINSTON. *(Recording.)* Hello. Winston again. It's eleven twenty. On Tuesday. And actually an email to cancel would've been good. I'm going to have to charge you for this one. Well. We can work something out.

(He sits and huffs for a second. Before. The tones of an outgoing call.)

A WOMAN'S VOICE. *(Recording.)* Hello?

WINSTON. *(Recording.)* Hi. Sorry. This is Winston Smith – calling for Matthew – we have an appointment today.

A WOMAN'S VOICE. *(Recording.)* Appointment?

(The recording becomes muffled as **WINSTON** *gets up and paces, leaving the recorder behind. In the office, they strain to hear. The feeling of not being able to look away from a train wreck.)*

WINSTON. *(Recording.)* Yes, an appointment with Matthew. Eleven on Tuesdays has been our usual slot. Is he around – available?

A WOMAN'S VOICE. *(Recording.)* Who are you?

WINSTON. *(Recording.)* Winston. Winston Smith. Who am I speaking to?

A WOMAN'S VOICE. *(Recording.)* This is Matthew's mum. He's not available – he's he's gone.

WINSTON. *(Recording.)* Gone?

    (Her voice cracks.)

A WOMAN'S VOICE. *(Recording.)* We we we found him last week.

WINSTON. *(Recording.)* Oh god.

Oh I'm so sorry.

I.

You found.

I'm so sorry for you. I mean, if I can do anything – anything at all –

A WOMAN'S VOICE. *(Recording.)* No, no – it's. It's fine. Goodbye.

WINSTON. *(Recording.)* Sorry. Goodbye.

    *(We hear some pacing before the recording is stopped. **CLAIRE** and **WINSTON** sit in the heaviness for a while. He composes himself.)*

CLAIRE. Are you alright?

WINSTON. Yes. Thank you.

CLAIRE. You need to disclose those.

WINSTON. Yes?

CLAIRE. I mean not disclosing them will only land you in more shit otherwise.

WINSTON. Do they. Help?

    (She thinks intently.)

CLAIRE. I think, amongst a lot of things, they show you had a genuine care for him.

WINSTON. I did. I do.

What happens now?

(*Beat. She stands and begins to move behind her desk.*)

CLAIRE. We dispute the claim. Go from there.

WINSTON. We? We. Okay. Thank you. And we're disputing?

(*Beat.*)

CLAIRE. Something.

WINSTON. Something.

CLAIRE. I think I can find something. Maybe.

WINSTON. Sure.

CLAIRE. Winston. I'll be risking something to do this with you. Okay?

WINSTON. I'll pay you.

CLAIRE. Of course you'll pay me. If I had the means, I'd make it extortionate. I'd rinse you.

I wasn't talking financially. Going back there...

WINSTON. I know. Thank you.

CLAIRE. Okay. Jesus. Okay. I'm going to have to listen again. I'm sorry, I won't make you go over it too many times.

WINSTON. It's okay.

(**CLAIRE** *readies herself. Hair up. Clearing the desk. As if to listen better. A new energy.*)

CLAIRE. What was the book going to be about?

WINSTON. The book? Oh. Making your life better using my methods. And well, yeah.

This might be the worst PR set up for a self-help book in fucking history.

CLAIRE. I think so.

> *(Despite everything, a smile.)*

You'll need to come back next week. I'll take the weekend and work something out.

WINSTON. Thank you thank you thank you.

CLAIRE. And are you. Okay?

WINSTON. Yes. Fine. Good. It'll be fine. Think positively.

CLAIRE. Right.

WINSTON. Exactly. Thank you, Claire.

CLAIRE. Shall we?

> *(He nods. The recording whirs and clicks back into starting position.)*

20.

JOY. Okay, okay I'm up – can you turn it off?

WINSTON. No. This is what a roadtrip is about. Singing along and having fun.

(**JOY** *turns down the music a little.*)

JOY. Question. If you – we – wanted to reconnect with, you know, the family on this side. Why didn't we go to find the Facebook sister. And that whole lot. In Swansea. If we don't find anyone, what then?

WINSTON. We're not from Swansea, Joy. We're from Mayo.

JOY. Okay. So. It's more about. Going to the place. Than. The people?

WINSTON. It's both.

JOY. What if we get there and don't find anyone? Sorry. Just worst case scenario.

WINSTON. I tell all my clients to always think 'best case scenario.' It's completely low vibrational to think of the worst. It just negates any chance of something good happening. Why can't you ever think 'best case scenario' –

JOY. Fine. Best case scenario we get there and

I dunno, yeah,

it's Bono.

WINSTON. Bono?

JOY. Yeah. He's your long lost family. Best case. There you go.

WINSTON. Bono – singular – is my entire long lost family. All of them.

JOY. Fine. Bono is your long lost dad.

WINSTON. I'm older than Bono.

JOY. Fine, he's fucking my long lost dad.

WINSTON. What does that make me then? Your best case scenario – let me get this right – is getting to Mayo and replacing me with Bono.

JOY. Right now? Yes.

WINSTON. Wow. Joy.

JOY. Sorry. Is that not how you envisioned me answering that question?

WINSTON. Best case scenario we all go with the flow and have an amazing time in Mayo on Buster and eat pies and feel connected to the place from whence we came and maybe meet some people with the same nose as us and although it'll be strange to see my nose on another man's face it'll make me feel like part of something. I'll get to stand on the grass or ground where a whole line of fathers and grandfathers and great grandfathers stood before me and breathe the same air as them and understand a bit more about why my father was the way that he was and why I am the way that I am and why the world works in the way that it does and ultimately why you are such a petulant fucking idiot to your father – who is not Bono – but is equally charismatic and philanthropic and actually Irish –

JOY. And worst case scenario?

WINSTON. I've messaged three people on Facebook, Joy. Everybody uses Facebook.

(*A beat.*)

We don't find anyone.

(Silence before the song changes and The Weather Girls begins to play.)*

*(**JOY** watches **WINSTON**'s stare determinedly ahead.)*

(Fuck it. With great effort, but little result, she attempts to sing along.)

WINSTON. Joy?

*(**JOY** continues to sing. **WINSTON** joins in.)*

WINSTON. We have fun, don't we, Joy?

JOY. Yes. We do.

WINSTON. We're not like the others / – See! This is fun! We're having fun! Turn it up!

*(**JOY** and **WINSTON** take it in turns, singing a line each. The duet grows louder as they reach the crescendo of the chorus together.)*

(As the bus drives under a bridge we hear a deafening elongated crash sound – the sound of metal ripping. Ideally, this will happen at the climax of the song –)

JOY. What the FUCK –

WINSTON. FUCK!

(The bus was one meter too high for the bridge and subsequently the bedroom ceiling and most of the bed now lies on the road. Big, handcrafted roadkill.)

FUCK fuck fuck fucking FUCK –

JOY. Oh my god. Oh my god.

---

*A licence to produce *Fatherland* does not include a performance licence for any third-party or copyrighted recordings. Licensees should create their own.

WINSTON. We're okay. We're okay. We're okay.

JOY. What was that?!

WINSTON. The roof –

JOY. The fucking roof!

Was anyone behind us?

WINSTON. No. We're okay. Jesus Christ.

JOY. I think I pissed myself – pull over! Oh my god/ Oh my god

WINSTON. I fucking am! Okay. Okay. Okay. Joy. Stop panicking. We need to cover the hole. The interior can't get wet.

JOY. Of course it's going to get wet – the bus is fucking roofless now –

WINSTON. There are electrical units on board – I'm going pick up the debris. There's a tent in that back cupboard – we're going to fix it like a tarpaulin –

JOY. Stop saying big words – what the fuck –

WINSTON. LISTEN TO ME AND GET THE FUCKING TENT.

(**WINSTON** *runs out into the road.*)

JOY. CAN WE NOT JUST CALL SOMEONE?

WINSTON. I CAN'T LEAVE BIG CHUNKS OF FUCKING METAL IN THE ROAD – SOMEONE COULD GET HURT /SERIOUSLY HURT.

JOY. I DON'T KNOW WHAT TO DO.

WINSTON. GET THE FUCKING TENT OUT! STOP WHINING AND DO WHAT I SAY!

(**JOY** *scrambles to find a tent in a cupboard. The Weather Girls sing relentlessly in the name of all that is camp.**)

(**WINSTON** *gathers up pieces of roof. A car passes and beeps.* **JOY** *untangles the tent.* **WINSTON** *runs back.*)

COME ON!

JOY. What do I use to – to – fix it –

WINSTON. Here!

JOY. My fucking hair!!

(*He finds a roll of gaffa tape –* **JOY** *stands on what's left of the bed and holds the tent above her head.*)

Just so you know – this is NOT fun –

WINSTON. Hold it tight. I'll tape it across.

JOY. I am NOT having a fun time –

WINSTON. Hold it!

JOY. I'm trying!

WINSTON. Try harder!

JOY. I cannot believe that you dragged me –

WINSTON. Higher! HIGHER!

JOY. – Did you not see the –

(*A car passes and beeps at them.*)

JOY & WINSTON. Oh fuck off!

---

* A licence to produce *Fatherland* does not include a performance licence for any third-party or copyrighted recordings. Licensees should create their own.

(**WINSTON** *lets out a noise – something primal, ballistic – rage and grief as he stands in the debris.*)

(*Blackout scored, still, by The Weather Girls.*[*])

---

[*] A licence to produce *Fatherland* does not include a performance licence for any third-party or copyrighted recordings. Licensees should create their own.

21.

*(Icicles form around the car, crowning the
wing mirrors.)*

JOY. everyone is screaming

scurrying

trying to hide

clawing at corners of the cage

the big latex hand scoops up a bunch of us

Tail first

we're all crammed together and it goes dark

Light. Harsh, bright light.

A new cage. Inside of it –

a green tube and a blue tube

at the other end of the blue – food

one by one we jump and crawl through the blue to
reach the food

it's a bit like PGL

They watch us and whisper

this all feels too easy

I see the blur of a white coat move towards us and they
take us somewhere else

it's cold here

Jump for blue – get the food

the temperature drops

Again and again

We shiver together

They murmur from above

I want to stop

my vision begins to blur

actually freezing now –

Go for blue – I think it was blue?

I look over at the rat to my side

he's walking in circles

hitting his head against the cage walls

A gloved hand reaches in and takes him

Another is chasing her own tail

or am I? I think I might be –

make it stop

I feel cold latex on my body and I pray to a rat god somewhere

please not me

please not me

please not fucking me

this is a fact

Scientists in the '80s, perms and big glasses,

i'm sure this is a fact, i read this somewhere? hypothermia on a group of rats, they watch them forget they watch all of them get colder, freeze up and forget

Like hitchhikers on Everest who take off all their clothes and lie down in the snow naked

i period the bed on tuesday and lie there for days willing myself to get up and wash but i can't remember a good enough reason to

22.

> (**JOY**, *utterly bedraggled by the crash, sits on the kerb. She finds a miraculously intact spliff in a pocket somewhere and lights it.*)

JOY. I want to go home.

> (**WINSTON** *stares, transfixed at the debris. The faint sound of breathing on the other end of a phone.*)

I want to go home. Dad.

> (**WINSTON** *bats away the noise.*)

WINSTON. And how do you suggest we do that? Will I just go back in time and change it? Will I just magically fucking un-crash it? What a good idea! Fuck, why hadn't I thought of that already!? Well, I can't. I can't change it. It's happened. It's all gone. Once something is gone it stays gone no matter how badly you wish it wasn't. And you live with it. Okay? Life goes on and you just try to live with it.

> (**JOY** *stares at him. He re-stacks himself. Shakes dirt off himself like a dog. Turns to* **JOY**, *sharp.*)

We could choose to laugh about this.

In fact, you could choose to laugh about something this whole trip.

JOY. I have been trying./You weren't laughing when it happened.

WINSTON. Have you? Blood from a fucking stone more like.

JOY. You shouted at me./ And it's not funny. It's dangerous –

WINSTON. It was a high pressure environment. When accidents happen/

JOY. It wasn't an accident. If you were paying attention. You'd have seen the sign on the bridge that clearly said if you're a big fucking bus –

WINSTON. You have eyes too – you should've seen it –

JOY. You're the driver and the grown up –

WINSTON. You're twenty seven –

JOY. I am twenty six.

WINSTON. Well, we used to be the fun ones. Me and you.

JOY. God, this is just a fucking disaster.

WINSTON. Is it? Really? I thought the cunting bridge destroying the product of months and months of my hard work was a good thing –

JOY. I shouldn't have come.

WINSTON. You wanted to get out of that flat.

JOY. No. I didn't at any point *want* to.

WINSTON. Well, next time say no.

JOY. I couldn't! I can't!

WINSTON. Of course you can.

JOY. No. I can't. We do things your way. I don't have a choice in it and when I do say I don't want to, we end up doing it anyway. So over time, I've learned it's more efficient to just go with it and cut out the part where we pretend that what I want matters. I'm not seven – you can't just bundle me up and put me in the back of the car! And we weren't 'the fun ones' I was a child. /You were a grown adult who I've since come to realise –

WINSTON. I am doing a nice thing. This is a nice thing.

JOY. For who?

WINSTON. For you! I mean, Mum said you were bad but I didn't expect the extent of this – moping around like a a a –

JOY. This isn't about me. I didn't want this!

WINSTON. I needed to – and you – you needed to get out – you've been all.

JOY. All what? Depressed. Yes. I have. I am. Life has been really shit recently. What with everything – with my job –

WINSTON. What what what job?

JOY. I stopped going! So there's that – and that paired with

Mum and then with. Him. Just. Shit. Shockingly shit. Rock bottom has a basement! And a wine cellar! And a –

WINSTON. I've asked you about all of this. Repeatedly. I have tried very fucking hard. Questions and questions about Mum and your your life and him – and you don't want to talk about it.

JOY. With you.

WINSTON. You've given me scraps –

JOY. I don't want to talk about it with you.

WINSTON. What is so terrible about me?

JOY. I'm not saying you're terrible –

WINSTON. You know I could help you. I'd try. I have years of experience coaching people.

JOY. Please – I am not one of your clients.

WINSTON. I'm not asking to be your life coach or therapist – I want to know what's going on in your life, especially if it's hurting you –

JOY. Trust me. I can't speak to you about this.

WINSTON. Why? Why not?

JOY. Because.

WINSTON. Because? Honestly, sometimes you can really over-dramatise things, Joy. Since you were little/

JOY. Fine. We've been looking at how I got here – every thing that happened –

every relationship and there's one common fucking denominator.

WINSTON. Go on.

JOY. You.

WINSTON. Right. How very convenient. Did she read psychiatry for idiot beginners, chapter one – Freud –

JOY. You left. And you'd come back for these weekends or surprises but everything was just completely drenched in chaos – and then you'd leave again –

WINSTON. You cannot blame me for everything –

JOY. And now I – because I don't know what it is to have a 'consistent male presence' – I either fuck something off before they can have a chance to leave me – Or I put up with scraps and I'm like fed off the chaos and drama of it – I'm not explaining it right –

WINSTON. No, you're not. Because it sounds like you're blaming me for every thing that's gone wrong in your life. Shit happens! Relationships end! People are bad! Instead of taking positive action and picking yourself up –

JOY. I'm not. But you use phrases like 'positive action' and – you know what – being really honest about everything –

WINSTON. Please.

JOY. I find it difficult to want to open up about the pain of being cheated on to someone who has done that to multiple women.

WINSTON. This is definitely from your mother.

JOY. Oh my god oh my god oh my god.

WINSTON. You know – things don't just happen to you, Joy – you get to decide when you stop letting shit just roll over you –

JOY. It's not from Mum. I'm not an idiot. I see things –

WINSTON. Do you? Have you asked me one question – one – about my life –

JOY. And it's not coincidental that I'm picking these shit men –

WINSTON. You're being ridiculous. And hurtful. And wallow-y/ And what the fuck is wrong with me being a life coach?

JOY. Wallowy isn't a word – There's nothing wrong with it/

WINSTON. I'm helping people!

JOY. Okay!

WINSTON. I am helping people change their lives and I want to help you –

JOY. I DON'T WANT YOUR HELP! I'm not another project! You helping me. I don't know. Will it be like the restaurant or the novel – sorry novels – or the word app being made in India – or the half painted bus with the toilet that doesn't really flush and the broken radio – You start A THOUSAND THINGS and we all have to invest in them and then suddenly they just disappear –

WINSTON. HEY IT'S MY LIFE AND MY CHOICES AND MY FUCKING BUS.

JOY. And sometimes it feels like I'm one of them and – and I'm just waiting for you to drop me again!

> (*A beat. The amber lights of a tow truck flash towards them.*)

This isn't about that. It's about. I don't know. I am not angry with you about that. I'm too tired to be angry about anything.

WINSTON. No. If I'm such an asshole – which I mean clearly I am – the mountains of evidence everybody seems to have to prove that – if I'm such a fuck up – then, please, don't let me stop you – go!

JOY. Dad.

WINSTON. But before you do –

JOY. I'm not –

WINSTON. Am I responsible for every shit thing that's gone on in your life or really, really – have you made some stupid fucking decisions and is it an easy direction to point the blame in? Word from the wise – or not so wise – you can't hate the roots without hating the fucking tree – and from the sounds of it you got some ugly feelings towards those roots of yours. So maybe/ look into that –

JOY. I don't hate you. You're projecting.

WINSTON. Someone's in therapy!

JOY. And being fucking mean.

WINSTON. You can get the train home if you want. I'm going to Mayo. I am following this through.

JOY. Fine!

> (**JOY** *leaves, slamming the door behind.*)

WINSTON. Don't slam the door!

JOY. Fuck your door!

WINSTON. I am helping people!

23.

*(**CLAIRE** turns on her heel towards **WINSTON**, energized.)*

CLAIRE. But you didn't!

WINSTON. What do you mean?

CLAIRE. So. Negligence implies you had a duty of care towards him. But, you're not a licensed physician or medical professional or caregiver –

WINSTON. I am a licensed life coach.

CLAIRE. Anyone can be. There's no specific training, educational backgrounds or licenses required by law. Anyone can call themselves a coach.

WINSTON. I suppose.

CLAIRE. Same as people who get ordained online and call themselves ministers without ever having been to Church.

WINSTON. Tempting.

CLAIRE. So. We lean into this. The fact you actually never had any concrete responsibility towards him or duty of care – 'negligence' implies you did, but actually, you didn't.

WINSTON. I mean.

CLAIRE. Yes, he was paying for a service from you, but he would've done the same for, I dunno, his hairdresser, but you weren't licensed to ever give medical advice or issue medicine or observe any kind of guidelines – anything that an actual *professional* would. So we can deny any claims of malpractice based on the idea that you –

WINSTON. Did nothing?

CLAIRE. Professionally speaking, yes.

WINSTON. Oh.

CLAIRE. What?

WINSTON. But I did. He was more confident and engaged and establishing goals.

CLAIRE. I'm sure.

WINSTON. I know that doesn't, you know, make sense now but I'm not just some – nothing – I'm not his hairdresser –

CLAIRE. I know. But we're denying their claim, which involves breaking down their claim into what it factually means and factually –

WINSTON. I was nothing. Professionally speaking.

CLAIRE. Yes.

(*Beat.*)

It's a way out, Winston. It's nothing groundbreaking. In fact, it was glaringly obvious when I thought about it. But it does mean they would fall at the first hurdle.

WINSTON. Then it'll be dropped?

CLAIRE. Well, not exactly. Probably. But they'll likely look at other legal options given their strength of feeling.

WINSTON. Lovely. Like what?

CLAIRE. Well. It's a guess but. Some form of manslaughter by coercive control.

WINSTON. Fucking hell, Claire!

CLAIRE. Which sounds bad.

WINSTON. Just a bit!

CLAIRE. But, it's much, much harder to prove. It would be a criminal case and I can't see the CPS ever bringing it.

Suicide ultimately can only be committed by the person who takes their own life. You'd have had to seriously encourage – coerce – almost force him into it. I've see a couple of cases in the States; partners or exes who send messages of encouragement to do – that – but very little similar here has succeeded. So, this would be some kind of first. Are you with me?

WINSTON. Yes.

CLAIRE. So, yes, we go through the sessions again and trust that they ultimately prove that you were a companion, a port of call, at a stretch – a friend for him. A good, reliable, responsible, compassionate one at that. Someone with their own children. It's how we present you.

WINSTON. Coercive...

CLAIRE. ...Manslaughter. Potentially. If they come back, that's what they'd come back with.

WINSTON. That's a big word.

24.

> (**JOY**, *alone. Snow falls in heavy cotton ball clumps around her.*)

JOY. I wish I had my fucking vape

Or a blanket

> (*Slowly, the snow begins to erase* **JOY***'s surroundings.*)

Or a blanket made of vapes

> (*Swirling masses, too thick, too furious and fast to track.*)

I should go

my teeth are no longer chattering and i'm not shivering

> (*Heavy, determined mounds of snow cement feet to the floor.*)

its like slipping into a warm bath

> (*The storm cradles her.*)

go, Joy, please, go

> (*We can barely see her through it now. And she can't see us.*)

drowsy and numbing and soothing and actually fucking delightful get up and move

go go go go go go

> (*More and more and more and.*)

in a minute

> (*White out.*)

25.

(Office. **CLAIRE***'s shoes are off.)*

WINSTON. You were right.

CLAIRE. Hm?

WINSTON. That they'd come back like this.

CLAIRE. At least we're prepared.

I didn't particularly want to be right.

WINSTON. They must really think I've done something.

CLAIRE. Or they're just really hurting. Grief makes you do things.

(Beat.)

WINSTON. I know.

CLAIRE. Is this all clear?

WINSTON. Perfectly.

CLAIRE. And you feel confident about it? What we're saying – what they could say?

WINSTON. Yes. Thank you.

CLAIRE. Well, I think that's everything we can do for now.

WINSTON. Okay then.

Are you nervous?

CLAIRE. No.

WINSTON. I won't think less of you if you are.

CLAIRE. I'm not. I trained for this. All those long nights and tests and no social life. It wasn't for nothing. I mean it also wasn't to get a group of fourteen-year-olds out of a lifelong ban from Wilkos for shoplifting.

Not actually a legal issue but they paid, so. But I feel really. Ready.

WINSTON. Why don't you do the juicy stuff then? Major fraud? Serial killers? Witch trials?

CLAIRE. I told you. Life got in the way.

WINSTON. Which bit of life?

CLAIRE. It wasn't just one bit.

> (**WINSTON** *holds her gaze.*)

It was a lot of things. So yeah. Then everything stopped. I stopped. And life – the life I thought I was going to have went on without me. So here I am.

WINSTON. You're too young to speak about life like that. All breathy. Like Meryl Streep.

CLAIRE. I'm not that young.

> (*Beat.*)

This has been good though.

I mean, not for you – it's been awful, but –

WINSTON. I know what you mean.

CLAIRE. All this to say, I think I feel…ready.

WINSTON. You could sound more believable!

CLAIRE. I feel ready. I am ready.

WINSTON. Good.

CLAIRE. And you?

WINSTON. I think you feel ready too.

CLAIRE. Call me if you have any questions. We'll meet before, nice and early. Don't be late. And I mean it, do call.

WINSTON. A question now.

CLAIRE. Go for it.

WINSTON. What do I wear for this sort of thing?

CLAIRE. No jokes on Monday. None. No matter how nervous.

WINSTON. I wouldn't. I won't. It is definitely the least funny thing that has ever happened to me.

CLAIRE. Good.

WINSTON. Thank you for everything. See you Monday.

CLAIRE. See you Monday.

Don't be late.

(Beat.)

WINSTON. I think of him all the time.

26.

*(White out. Everything new, untouched. Joy
looks out at this sea of white.)*

JOY. Solstice actually comes from solstitium – latin for
stands still. Knowing the origin of a word is good for
you.

Sol – stitium. As in the sun appears to stand still in the
sky for a day and a night.

For a day and a night, each year, after weeks and weeks
of getting colder and darker, we stop.

Then, we move again. This time away from the sun
but towards longer days, shorter nights, – after an
interminable wait, we move towards heat and warmth
and short sleeves and green shoots.

I want to dream about sunrise at stone henge

about harvest

and pomegranates and persimmons and watermelon
eaten with sticky fingers

I want to shut my eyes and call in spring

27.

(**WINSTON**, *alone in the drivers seat. Still no sign of* **JOY**. *Still no sign of Dave. He toys with his phone. Goes back and forth.*)

VOICEMAIL. Your inbox is full. To hear your messages, press one.

(*A few beeps as he deletes them, pausing at the last one –*)

CLAIRE. *(Voicemail.)* Are you fucking KIDDING me, Winston? Seriously. I've never found myself wishing some kind of car accident on someone like this before – not because I'm wishing pain or death upon you but because you better have a fucking good excuse at hand!

I'm stood there – back in those offices – in front of that whole lot and I kept on vouching for you – "he's coming, he's coming" –

like an idiot – honestly, I have never been this humiliated –

his poor fucking mother, stood there – waiting too –

(*He hangs up. Let's whatever this feeling is wash over him; grisly, murky and familiar all at once. It comes in waves. At best, it foams up onto an unwelcome shore, frothing away. And at worst, it's huge cacophonous turbulent waves pulling at him; down, down, down.*)

(**JOY**'s discarded vape sits on the dashboard. He gives it a puff. Sickly sweet fog clogs his throat, he splutters, coughs, heaves in a fit, and at some point the wave inside him breaks.*)

(*He taps clunkily on his phone. We hear the dial tones of an outgoing call.*)

JOY. Hello?

WINSTON. Hi.

    (A beat.)

I was. Some kind of beast. They should keep me in a cage in a lab and do experiments on me to work out why I'm so. Beastly.

JOY. It's okay.

WINSTON. A small dingy lab with really sadistic scientists.

    (A pause.)

I'm sorry about the bus.

JOY. It was a good bus.

WINSTON. She was okay.

JOY. Will she survive?

WINSTON. In Dave's Mechanics we trust.

    (A pause.)

Are you coming back?

JOY. No.

WINSTON. I can come and pick you up from somewhere.

JOY. You can't. Your bus is fucked.

WINSTON. Hey. It's a convertible now.

JOY. No roof, no problem.

WINSTON. Daddy cool.

I'll hire a car. From Dave.

JOY. Dave this, Dave that. It's okay.

WINSTON. Okay.

JOY. I feel bad too. About the things I said.

WINSTON. We all say things we don't mean in the heat of it.

JOY. No, I feel bad because I meant them. Some of them anyway.

    (A pause.)

WINSTON. Joy. I have a whole book of things I wish I'd said to people. Your mum, your sister, my mother, my father, a barista I made cry – lots of unsaid things past their expiration date. And you look back and just think why didn't I just say something.

In fact. Perhaps now is the perfect time to say it. To you.

I know how heavy it can all get. I do. But, if I look back to when I was twenty seven.

JOY. Twenty six.

WINSTON. God. I was a baby. I had so many more places to see and people to meet and I hadn't had you or your sister – I hadn't met your mother – I hadn't met Nicole – or Lesley or – or –

JOY. Marianne.

WINSTON. Yes! Marianne. God. Always forget about her. There were so many people left for me to love. These big life changing love stories that I had no idea were coming.

And I wish I could tell that young man what was in store. To just hold on a bit longer and see what's round the corner.

JOY. That's a nice sentiment. Really nice.

WINSTON. It's the truth. I'm sorry about all of this. I'm sorry about the bastards. I'm sorry that I've been the bastard now and again.

JOY. It's okay.

WINSTON. And I'm sorry about the roof.

JOY. You said that. Hey, everything is copy.

WINSTON. I like that. Where's that from? Everything is copy. Maybe I should write a film about this.

JOY. That was more of a turn of phrase not a suggestion –

WINSTON. I've always wanted to write a film.

Or a podcast. How do you feel about podcasts?

JOY. Badly. I feel badly about them.

WINSTON. We could have one together.

JOY. Write the film. Fix the bus. Then write the film.

WINSTON. Oh bollocks. Yes.

JOY. What are you going to do?

WINSTON. I have to get back. Poorly planned trip on my part – no surprises there. Got to see Nicole. Sort some stuff. Bla bla bla. See if I can salvage Buster and then back to it.

(A beat.)

Joy. I.

JOY. What?

WINSTON. No. It's nothing. I need to ask something of you.

JOY. Go for it.

WINSTON. It's. You know me. I can get myself into. How did you put it. Things?

JOY. Lots of things. Yeah.

WINSTON. Well. That's the thing. I. Was going to ask you.

Will you forgive me for the *Happy Feet* thing?

JOY. Sure. Was that it?

WINSTON. Yes. No. I. Well.

Bloody bank has fucked up. So. So.

I need to borrow some money.

JOY. Okay.

WINSTON. I'm sorry.

JOY. Don't be.

WINSTON. You don't have your games job.

JOY. I have savings.

WINSTON. I'll pay you back.

JOY. For a rainy day.

WINSTON. Torrential, darling.

JOY. Why don't you ask –

WINSTON. I think I see Dave coming now.

JOY. I'll let you go then.

WINSTON. He's only twelve hours late.

JOY. Text me your details and what you need and I'll send it.

WINSTON. Thank you.

JOY. It's okay. Yeah. Just text me.

WINSTON. Will do. Will you get home safely?

JOY. I'll try. Love to Dave. Bye.

WINSTON. Bye, sweetheart.

(A beat.)

JOY. I'll let you know if I see Bono.

WINSTON. What? You're going?

JOY. I'm going.

(*A small laugh from* **JOY**.)

WINSTON. There she is. My Joy.

(**JOY** *hangs up. We see her.*)

(*She stands on the deck of the ferry, the salt of the Irish Sea in the air, a slither of sunlight piercing through the grey.*)

//

(**CLAIRE** *stands outside of the shitty office in Bristol, smoking.*)

(**WINSTON** *appears in front of her.*)

(**CLAIRE** *takes him in. The dirt, debris and exhaustion.*)

(*They hold each others gaze for a while. Then, she stubs out her cigarette and walks back inside.*)

(*Beat.*)

(**WINSTON** *follows.*)

//

(*A loud horn sounds as the boat pull out of the port.*)

(**JOY** *begins to thaw.*)

(*Go go go go. Onwards.*)

The End

Number of vehicle collisions with the railway bridge over Victoria Road in Gowerton:

2008 – 3 times
2009 – 3 times
2010 – 7 times
2011 – 2 times
2013 – 2 times
2014 – 1 time
2015 – 6 times
2016 – 1 time
2017 – 2 times
2018 – 1 time
2019 – 2 times
2020 – 3 times

ABOUT THE AUTHOR

Nancy Farino is a writer and actor from the West Midlands. She trained at The Bristol Old Vic Theatre School and has since worked as an actor with Netflix, Apple, BBC and Sky.

She began co-writing and producing plays in 2017.

Her theatre work includes *Twenty Something* (Old Red Lion/Edinburgh Fringe Festival) and *Blessings* (Camden Peoples Theatre).

Alongside this, she has been developing her latest play, *My Strong Intent*, as part of Hampstead's Inspire Programme.

9 780573 000942